SHERGOOD PUBLISHING
6040 E. Main Street, Suite 134
Mesa, Arizona 85205, USA

First Published in the United States of America by Shergood Publishing 2012

Copyright © David Negrette, 2012
All rights reserved

http://shergoodpublishing.com

# Table of Contents

Introduction .................................................................................................. 3
1. The OneNote Paradigm ........................................................................ 4
2. Setting up Your "Getting Things Done" Notebook ....................... 5
3. Setting Up Your Buckets ...................................................................... 7
4. Setting Up Your Action Categories ................................................... 8
5. Setting up Your In-basket ................................................................... 10
    To Be Processed ..................................................................................... 10
6. Processing Your In-basket ................................................................. 11
    Trash ........................................................................................................ 12
    Incubate .................................................................................................. 13
    Reference ................................................................................................ 15
    Projects ................................................................................................... 16
    Project Plans .......................................................................................... 19
    Waiting ................................................................................................... 20
    Calendar ................................................................................................. 21
    Next Actions .......................................................................................... 25
7. Wrapping Up ........................................................................................ 26
8. Done For You GTD Notebook Template ........................................ 27
Other Books from Shergood Publishing ............................................. 28

# Introduction

David Allen's *Getting Things Done: The Art of Stress-Free Productivity* was first published in 2001. When I read it in 2012, I wondered if any software had come along since then that might have revolutionized the core 5-step process. I experimented with the latest versions of word processors, spreadsheets, calendars, email clients, and even the popular EverNote app. Some of them made the process easier in one way or another, but none of them was the Holy Grail that I was looking for.

I recently upgraded to Windows 8 and noticed the icon that had appeared on my new start screen. I'd seen various versions of it on my computers for years but had ignored it. Everybody else I knew had ignored it as well. For some reason, perhaps because of my experiments with EverNote, I thought of the GTD system. "Hmm. What if…"

The rest is history. My experiments with collecting and organizing my workflow with Microsoft OneNote were a tremendous success. The software could do anything I wanted to do and more. I was amazed at how flexible and powerful it was, and even more so by the fact that so many people have it and ignore it without any inkling of its potentially life-changing capability.

I wrote this book to show you how to set up Microsoft OneNote for use with David Allen's Getting Things Done system. In doing so, I'm assuming that you have read his book and are familiar with it. It's not required, but you'll have a far better understanding of what I'm doing here if you are.

If you have a recent version of Microsoft Office, you will most likely have Microsoft OneNote on your system. It also comes with Windows tablets and Windows phones. If, by some chance, you discover that you don't have OneNote, you can buy it as a stand-alone product at a fairly reasonable price.

For your convenience, here are Amazon links to David Allen's book and the OneNote software:

Getting Things Done: The Art of Stress-Free Productivity

Microsoft OneNote 2010

# 1. The OneNote Paradigm

Microsoft OneNote is based on a *notebook* paradigm. When you create a notebook, you can add an unlimited number of *sections*. Each section can have an unlimited number of *pages*. Each page can have an unlimited number of *notes*.

The notebook hierarchy looks like this:

**Notebook**
    **Sections**
        **Pages**
            **Notes**

This is what it looks like in OneNote:

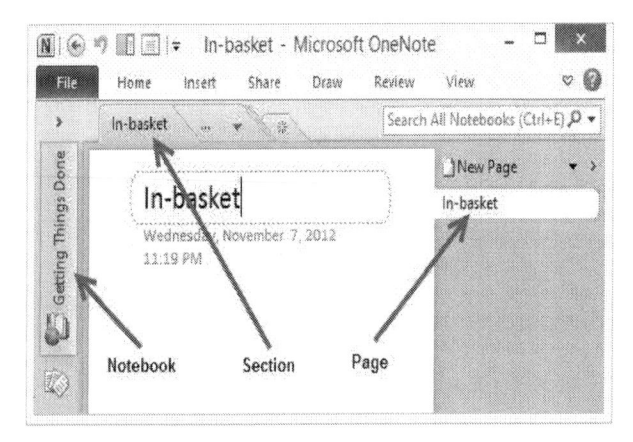

**Figure 1: The Notebook Hierarchy**

Each page can contain any number of the following note types:

- Audio Recordings
- File Attachments
- File Printouts
- Hyperlinks
- Pictures
- Plain Text
- Scanned Printouts
- Screen Clips
- Tables
- Video Recordings
- Web Clips

This gives you a great deal of flexibility in how you can manage your "stuff". We'll show you one way to do it in the following chapters.

## 2. Setting up Your "Getting Things Done" Notebook

Setting up your new GTD notebook is fast and easy. Here's what you do:

1. Click the **File** tab and select **New**.
2. Select the storage option for your notebook. We highly recommend that you use the web option so that you can access your GTD list from other PCs, tablets, and smart phones. If you don't have a free SkyDrive account, OneNote will walk you through the process of setting one up in your web browser.
3. Give your new notebook a relevant name like "Getting Things Done" or "GTD". If there will be someone else using OneNote in your file space, you might want to give it a more personal name like "Ralph's GTD".
4. Choose the specific file location for your storage option.
5. Click the "**Create Notebook**" button at the bottom.

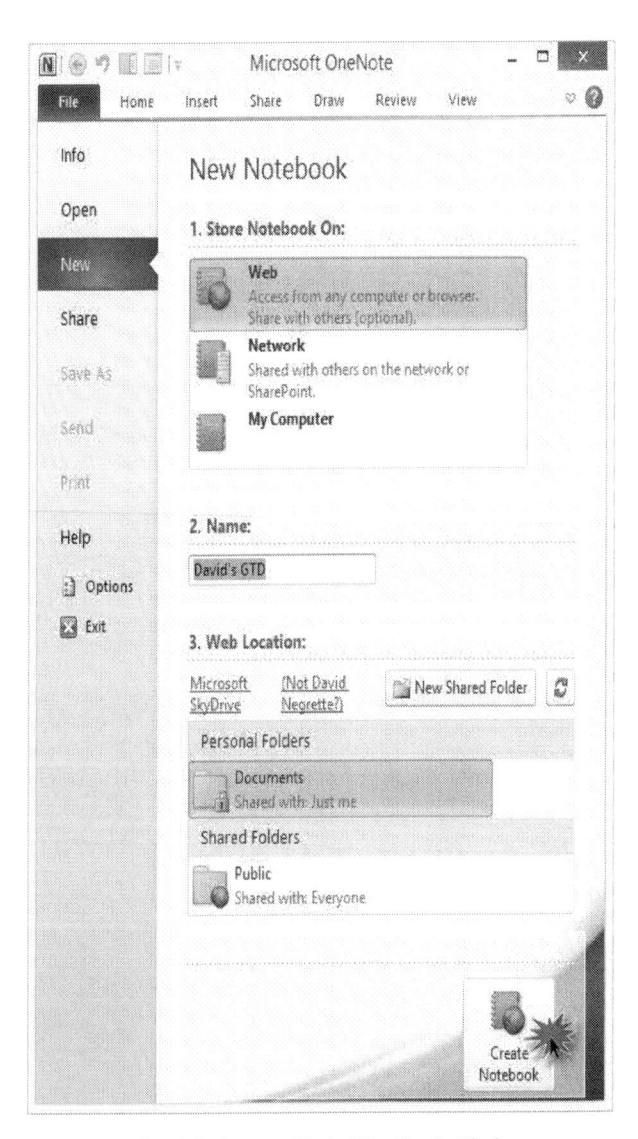

Figure 2: Setting up your "Getting Things Done" notebook

# 3. Setting Up Your Buckets

In the OneNote paradigm, your buckets will be contained in sections of your notebook. These are the tabs that run along the top of your pages. We're also going to include an **In-basket** so that we have a digital repository for your physical in-basket. As a result, these are the buckets that you'll want to set up in your notebook:

1. In-basket
2. Trash
3. Incubate
4. Reference
5. Projects
6. Project Plans
7. Waiting
8. Calendar
9. Next Actions

You can create new section tabs by clicking the * tab at the end of the tab row. Change the section name to your bucket name. The big dashed oval is for your page title. You can use the bucket name there as well. Go ahead and create all 9 sections now.

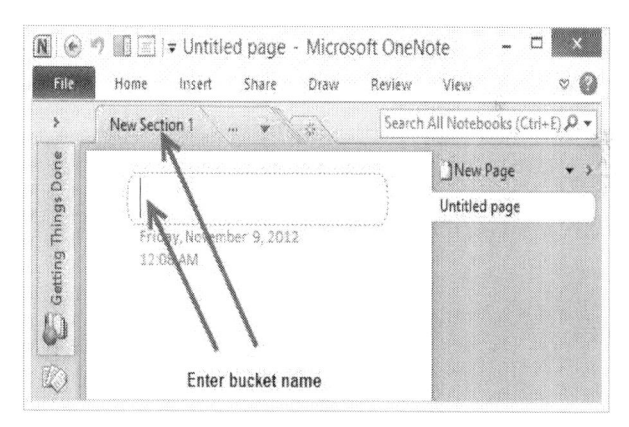

Figure 3: Setting up a bucket

If necessary, you can rename your sections by right-clicking the tab and selecting **Rename**.

## 4. Setting Up Your Action Categories

The final thing we need to do is to set up the action categories for organizing your action lists. This is also very easy to do in OneNote and will only take a few minutes. Below are the common categories from David Allen's book. Start with these and modify or add to them as necessary:

1. Agendas
2. At Computer
3. At Home
4. At Office
5. Calls
6. Errands
7. Read / Review

In the OneNote paradigm, these action categories are called **tags**. Whenever you want to add an item to an action list, you simply add an OneNote tag. Here's how you set them up:

1. On the **Home** tab, click the **Tag** button and select **Customize Tags...** at the bottom.
2. In the Customize Tags pop-up window, click **New Tag...**
3. In the **New Tag** pop-up window, enter a display name.
4. Choose a symbol, font color, and highlight color.
5. Click **OK** in the New Tag window.
6. Click **OK** in the Customize Tags window.

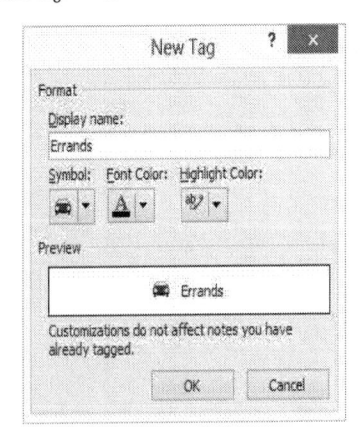

Figure 4: Setting up action categories (tags)

Notice how your new tags have populated at the top of the **Customize Tags** window. They've also been assigned a shortcut key. You can change their order by selecting them and using the **up** and **down** buttons to the right. Here's one way that you might set them up:

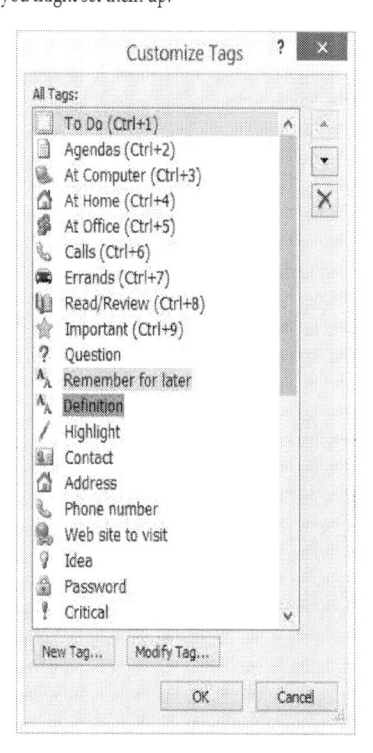

Figure 5: An example of how you might order your tags

Believe it or not, your new digital "Getting Things Done" productivity system is now set up and ready to go!

# 5. Setting up Your In-basket

Your new digital in-basket is going to be the core of your productivity system. Managing it efficiently will be critical to your success. Fortunately, the power of OneNote makes it easy.

As with most things, the key to your success will be to keep it simple. Your In-basket will contain just one thing: **a simple list of everything that has recently come to your attention**. The oldest items should be at the top, the newest at the bottom.

## To Be Processed

This is the only thing you'll have in your in-basket.

1. Place your cursor near the top of the page and type "**To Be Processed**".
2. Highlight your new title. A context menu will fade in.
3. Select a bigger font and bold it.
4. Go to the next line and right-click. The context menu will fade in.
5. Select the normal font and style.
6. Press enter to create a blank line.
7. Enter all of the open issues that currently have your attention, one per line.

**To Be Processed**

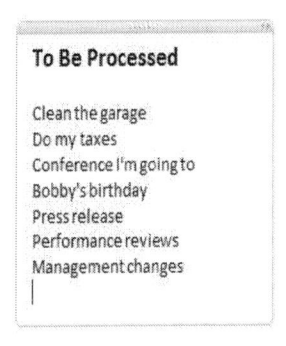

Clean the garage
Do my taxes
Conference I'm going to
Bobby's birthday
Press release
Performance reviews
Management changes

Figure 6: An initial "To Be Processed" list

That's it. Your new in-basket is ready to be processed.

## 6. Processing Your In-basket

According to David Allen in chapter 6 of *Getting Things Done: The Art of Stress Free Productivity*, there are five possible results from the processing phase:

1. An item goes into the trash.
2. An item gets completed because it takes less than two minutes to complete.
3. An item gets delegated to somebody else.
4. An item gets placed into one of your other buckets.
5. An item gets escalated into a multi-step project.

Here are some suggestions on to how to perform this process in Microsoft OneNote productivity system:

## Trash

During the processing phase, you might choose to send an item to the **Trash** bucket for one or more of the following reasons:

- The item is not actionable.
- The item contains no actions that you should be the one to perform.
- The item is not sufficiently important to spend any time on.

To permanently trash an item:

1. Highlight the item.
2. Press the **Del** key.

To temporarily trash an item:

1. Highlight the item.
2. Press **Ctrl-C**.
3. Click on the **Trash** tab.
4. Place the cursor in the desired location on the page.
5. Press **Ctrl-V**.
6. Press **space bar, hyphen, space bar**.
7. On the **Insert** menu, click **Time Stamp → Date & Time**.

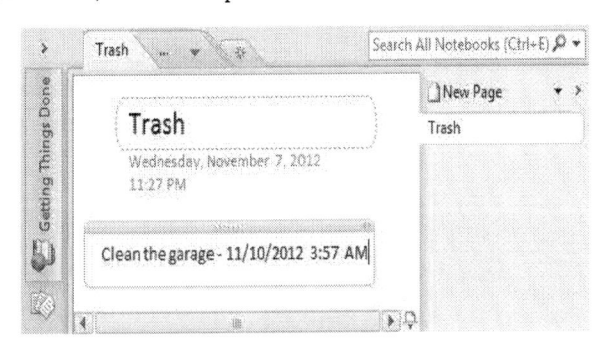

Figure 7: Trash item with time stamp

## Incubate

During the processing phase, you might say to yourself, "There's nothing to do on this now, but there might be later." Those items will go into your **Incubate** bucket.

Since there are no action items involved, entries will be moved to the **Incubate** bucket exactly the same way that we moved them to the Trash tab:

1. Highlight the item.
2. Press **Ctrl-C**.
3. Click on the **Trash** tab.
4. Place the cursor in the desired location on the page.
5. Press **Ctrl-V**.
6. Press **space bar, hyphen, space bar**.
7. On the **Insert** menu, click **Time Stamp → Date & Time**.

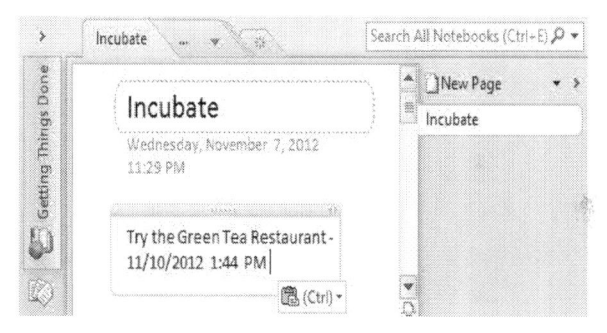

Figure 8: Incubate item with time stamp

You can also use Microsoft OneNote's powerful features to add tables, images, screen captures, hyperlinks, file attachments, scanned documents, audio recordings, and video recordings to your entries. Just go to the **Insert** menu after you paste your item.

In this case we'll add a scanned image from a flyer we got in the mail:

1. Go to the **Insert** menu
2. Click the **Scanner Printout** icon in the files section

Figure 9: Incubator entry with scanned flyer

## Reference

From time to time, you may run across useful information about some of the projects or topics that you're tracking. Microsoft OneNote is great at holding any information that you can digitize. The challenge is in keeping it organized.

Here's one simple way of managing your Reference bucket:

Create a page for each topic or project that you find information for. Here's an example of what that might look like:

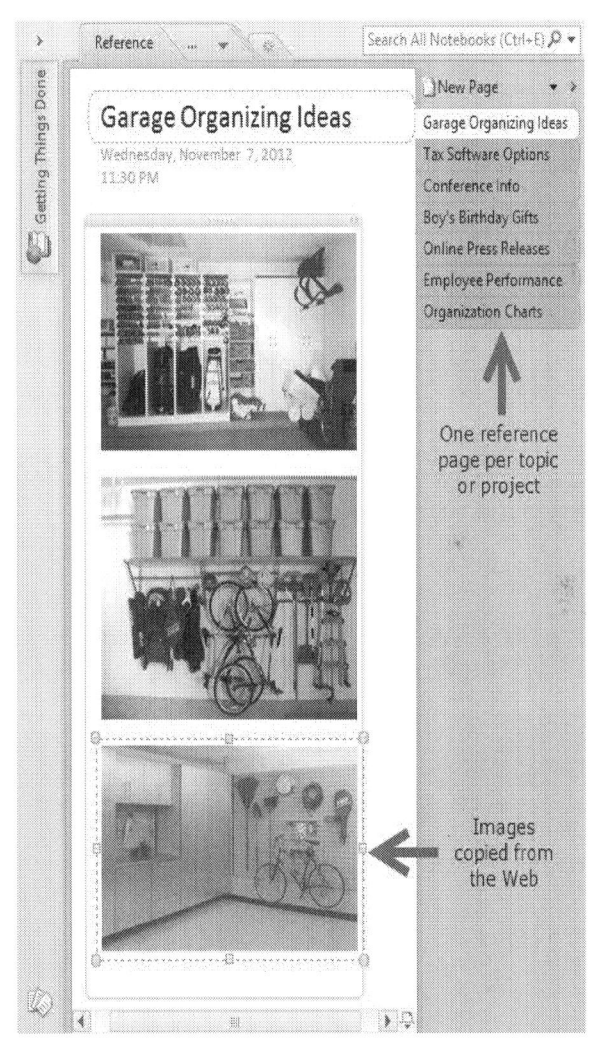

Figure 10: Images used as reference material

You might also want to add time stamps, text descriptions, or links to images that you copy.

## Projects

Many of the items in your In-basket will require multiple action steps. The **Projects** bucket will be your master list.

When you identify projects during your review process, you'll simply move them from your In-basket to your **Projects** bucket and add a checkbox. You can also add a category tag if you wish.

Here's how you do it:

Move multi-step items from your In-basket to your **Projects** bucket (make sure you delete them from your In-basket):

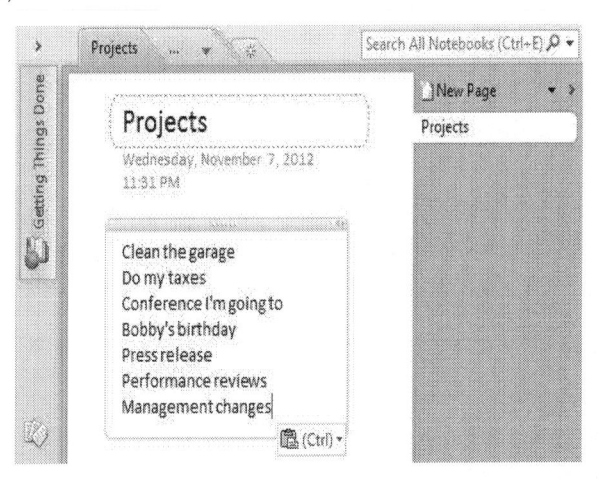

Figure 11: Items moved from in-basket

Add boxes to check when the entire project has been completed by going to the **Home** menu and selecting **Tag** → **To Do**:

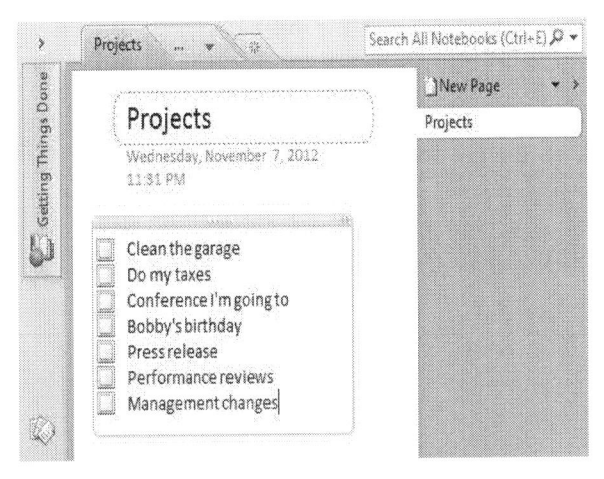

*Figure 12: Project list with checkboxes*

Add category tags by going to the **Home** menu and selecting **Tag** → **<category>**:

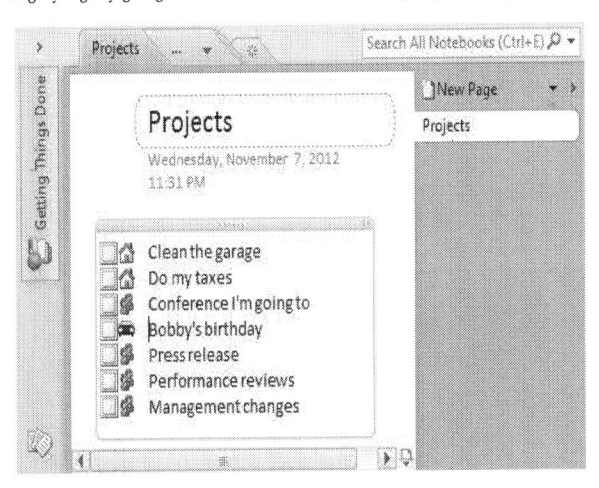

*Figure 13: Project list with checkboxes and tags*

You can add multiple category tags to any project if you wish.

At some point, you may want to divide your projects into categories. You can do this by moving categories to different frames and adding a text label at the top of each one:

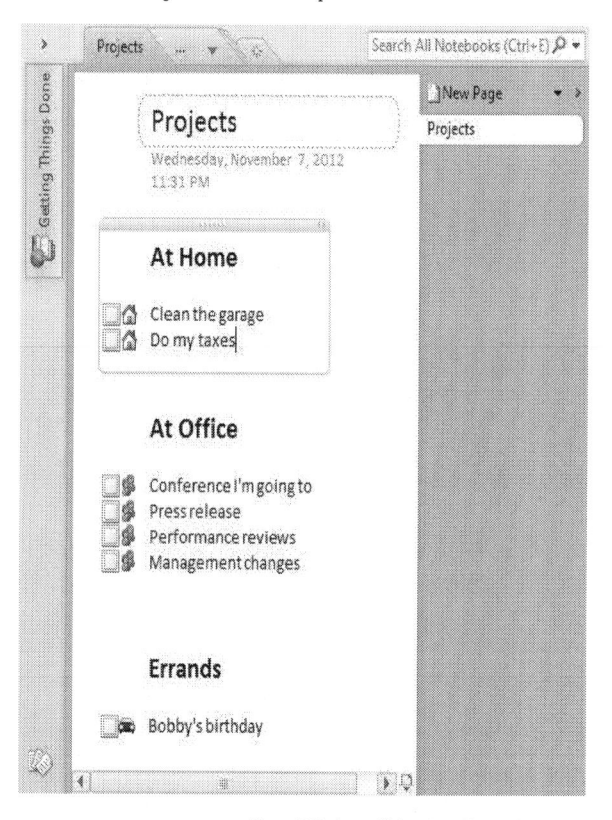

**Figure 14: Projects split into categories**

It's very important that you keep all of your projects "above the fold" (visible on the screen without scrolling). If necessary, put your lists in a two-column format to keep them easily visible. The frames containing your lists can be arranged side-by-side as well as top-to-bottom.

## Project Plans

The **Project Plans** bucket is the area where you'll break down your projects into individual actions. It's important that you don't try to list ALL of the actions required to complete each project. You should only list the NEXT action. If that action will take less than two minutes, you should do it, check it off, time stamp it, and then list the action to perform after that.

You should immediately do one of the following for your next action in each project plan:

1. Delegate the task to someone else.
2. Place the task onto your calendar to do at a specific time.
3. Place the task onto your Next Actions list.

After doing so, the task should be copied to the appropriate bucket in your Microsoft OneNote GTD system.

Each project in your **Projects** section should have its own page in your **Project Plans** section.

Here's an example of what your **Project Plans** section might look like:

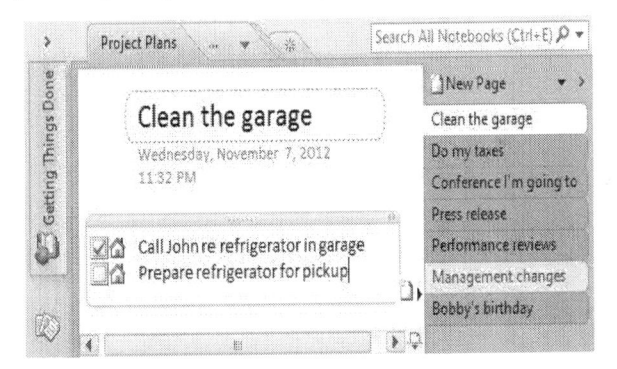

Figure 15: A sample Project Plans section – only the next action is listed

Just as with your Projects section, it's important that all tasks be "above the fold." Note how your other projects are also easily visible in the page list on the right.

## Waiting

If the next action is going to take longer than two minutes, ask yourself, "Am I the best person to be doing it?" If not, hand it off to the appropriate party and move it to your **Waiting** bucket.

Items in the **Waiting** bucket will either be new single-step action items from your **In-basket**, or actions that you choose to delegate from your **Project Plans** bucket. For these items, you may want to add an assignment date (consider using the time stamp feature) and a due date.

Depending on how many items you have delegated at any one time, you can use either titled sections on a single page or individual pages for each topic or project.

Here's an example of what your **Waiting** section might look like:

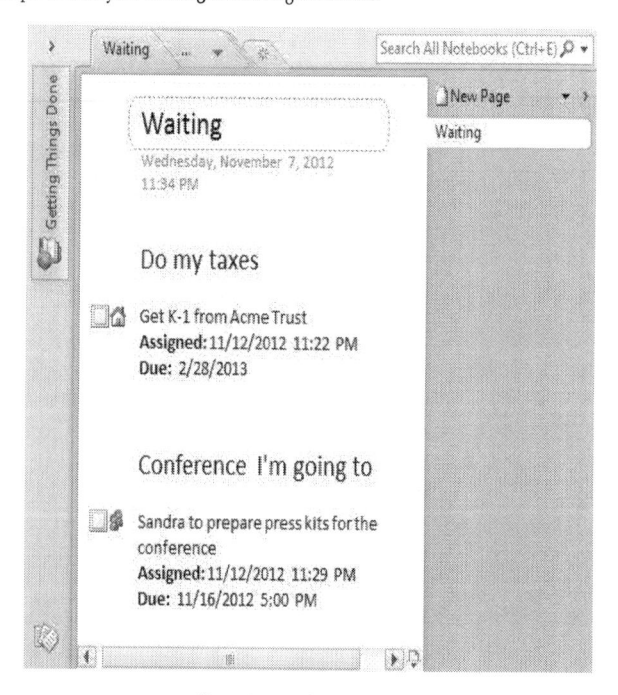

Figure 16: A sample Waiting section

## Calendar

Your next actions will often have to be performed at a specific time. These should be written in your calendar. You can also copy the appointment to your Calendar bucket for tracking within your Microsoft OneNote GTD system.

Items in the **Calendar** bucket will either be new single-step action items from your **In-basket**, or actions that you choose to delegate from your **Project Plans** bucket. For these items, you may want to add the date and time that the item is scheduled for in your calendar.

Depending on how many items you have on your calendar at any one time, you can use either titled sections on a single page or individual pages for each topic or project.

Here's an example of what your **Calendar** section might look like:

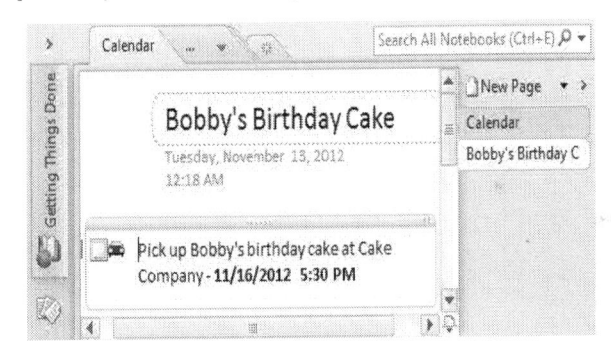

Figure 17: A sample Calendar section

If you happen to use Microsoft Outlook as your calendar, then you have an additional option: Linked Meeting Notes.

Here's how to copy a calendar entry from Microsoft Outlook to Microsoft OneNote:

1. Open an appointment and click the Linked Meeting Notes icon:

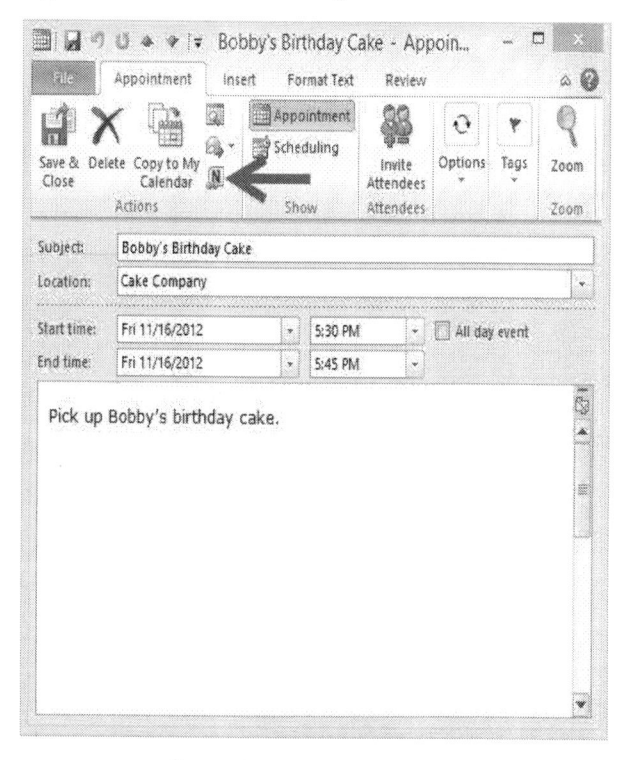

Figure 18: Click the Linked Meeting Notes icon

Select the Calendar section of your GTD notebook:

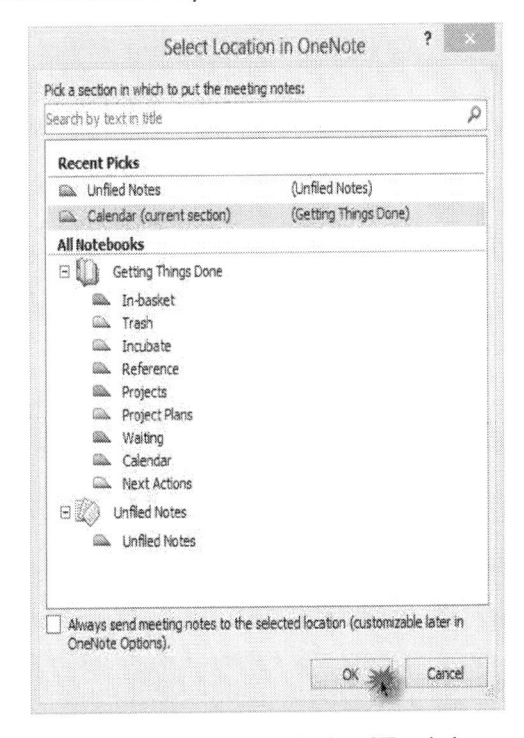

Figure 19: Select the Calendar section of your GTD notebook

Here's what your linked calendar entry might look like:

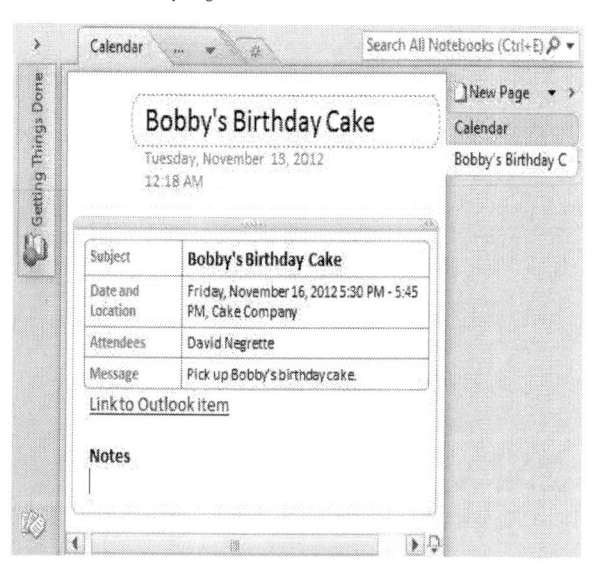

Figure 20: A sample linked calendar section entry

## Next Actions

The **Next Actions** bucket is for next action items that:

- Will be performed by you
- Are not part of a project (stand-alone)
- Can't be set for a specific date or time

Depending on how many items you have delegated at any one time, you can use either titled sections on a single page or individual pages for each topic or project.

Here's an example of what your **Next Actions** section might look like:

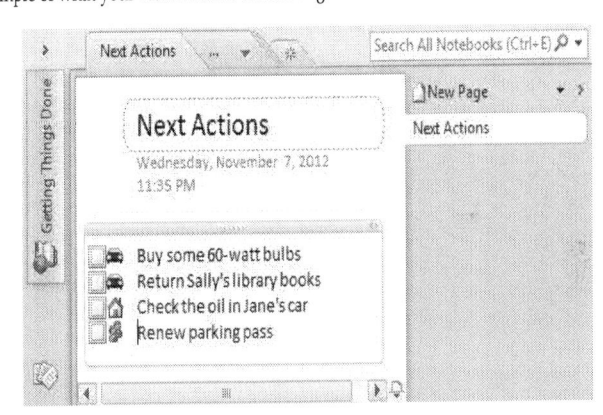

Figure 21: Sample Next Actions section

# 7. Wrapping Up

That's all, folks! You now have all the tools you need to implement David Allen's Getting Things Done productivity system with Microsoft OneNote.

You should view what you learned here as a foundation upon which you can build a custom GTD productivity system tailored for your individual needs. Once you become familiar with this system and the power of Microsoft OneNote software, you'll undoubtedly come up with new ideas to try.

Feel free to explore and test. The only thing you can do wrong is not to use any productivity system at all.

We hope you'll enjoy the productivity boost that using Microsoft OneNote will bring you.

## 8. Done For You GTD Notebook Template

If you'd like to download an empty Getting Things Done notebook for Microsoft OneNote that you can jump in and start using right away, you can download it from the following link:

http://shergoodpublishing.com/getting-things-done-template

## Other Books from Shergood Publishing

Do you have trouble relaxing? Try this book with descriptions of 50 peaceful scenes to enhance your visualization and relaxation skills:

**Seeds of Comfort**

Made in the USA
Lexington, KY
04 May 2013